Rookie
Read-About® Science

Looking Through a Microscope

By Linda Bullock

Consultants
David Larwa
National Science Consultant

Nanci R. Vargus, Ed.D.
Assistant Professor of Literacy
University of Indianapolis
Indianapolis, Indiana

Children's Press®
A Division of Scholastic Inc.
New York   Toronto   London   Auckland   Sydney
Mexico City   New Delhi   Hong Kong
Danbury, Connecticut

Designer: Herman Adler Design
Photo Researcher: Caroline Anderson
The photo on the cover shows a child looking through a microscope.

Library of Congress Cataloging-in-Publication Data

Bullock, Linda.
  Looking through a microscope / by Linda Bullock.
      p. cm. – (Rookie read-about science)
  Summary: Simple text and photographs describe and illustrate how to use
  a microscope.
    ISBN 0-516-22872-2 (lib. bdg.)   0-516-27912-2 (pbk.)
    1. Microscopes–Juvenile literature. 2. Microscopy–Juvenile
  literature. [1. Microscopes. 2. Microscopy.] I. Title. II. Series.
    QH211.B76 2003
    502'.8'2–dc21
                                                2003000465

CHILDREN'S PRESS, and ROOKIE READ-ABOUT®,
and associated logos are trademarks and or registered trademarks
of Scholastic Library Publishing. SCHOLASTIC and associated logos
are trademarks and or registered trademarks of Scholastic Inc.

1 2 3 4 5 6 7 8 9 10 R 12 11 10 09 08 07 06 05 04 03

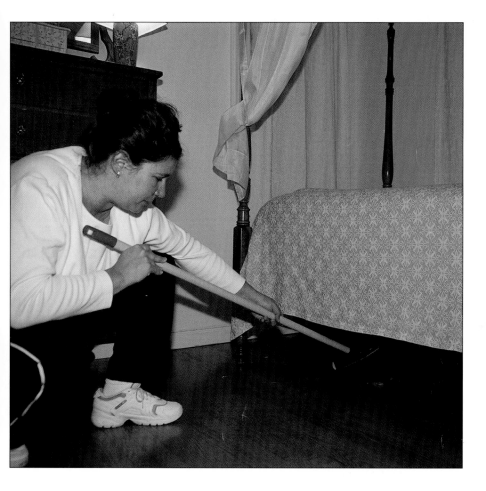

What is hiding under
your bed?

It is a dust ball. On the outside, it is soft and gray.

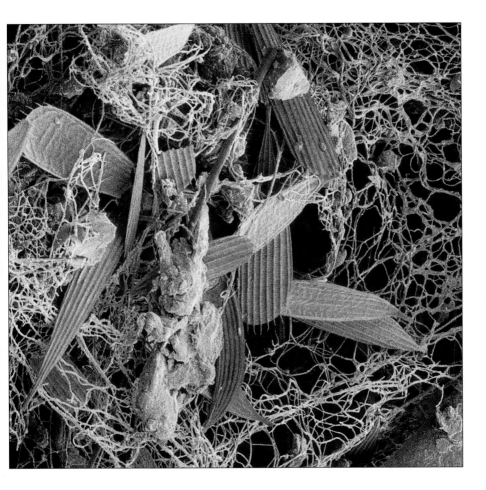

Inside, there is much
more to see.

What is inside a ball of dust? How can you know? You can use a microscope (MYE-kruh-skope).

A microscope is a science
(SYE-uhnss) tool.

It makes small things
look bigger.

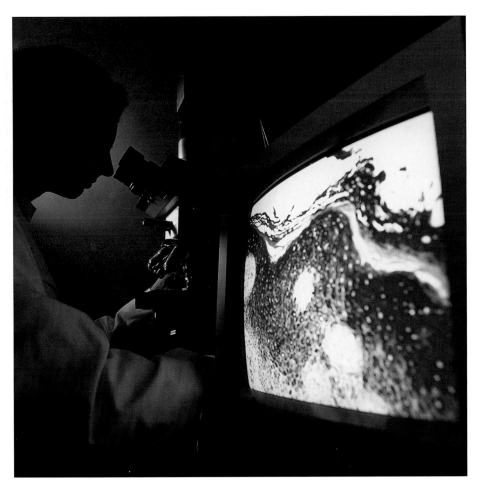

A microscope lets us see things we can't see using just our eyes.

We can look close.

Then we can look closer.

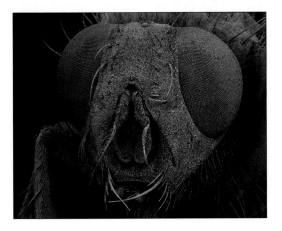

A microscope lets us see
what is in a dust ball.
There are hairs from a dog.

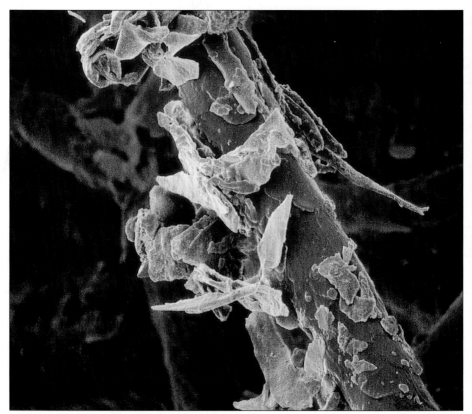

Dog hair

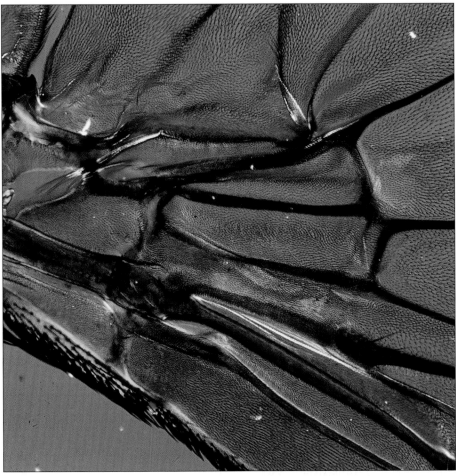

A fly's wing

There are bits of insect wings.

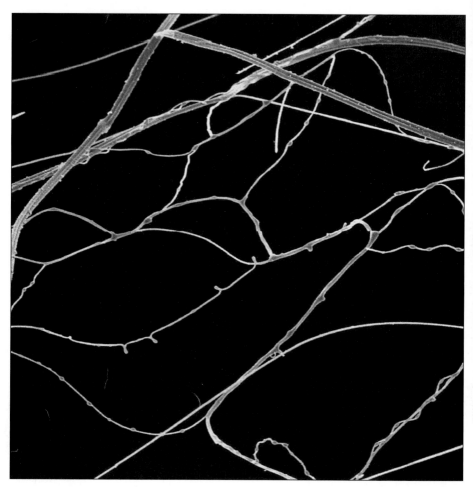

Spider web

There are bits of a spider web.

A relative of the spider
may be in the dust, too.
It is called a dust mite.

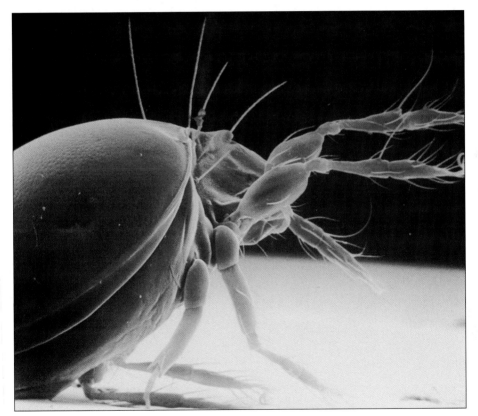

Dust mite

Dust mites are tiny animals. They eat flakes of skin. These flakes fall from your body.

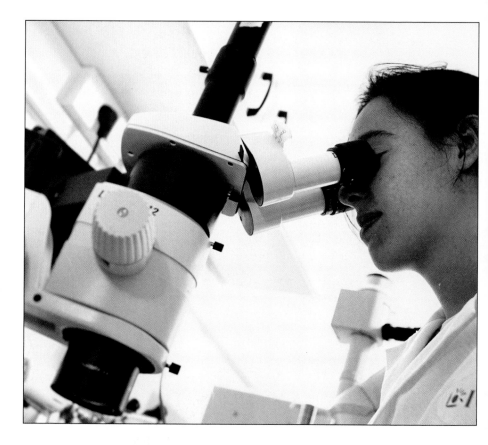

Many people use
microscopes at work.
Doctors use them.

They look for germs that
make you sick.

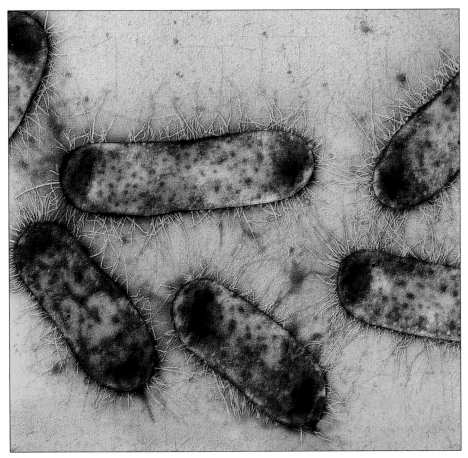

Germs

People use microscopes to help solve crimes. Microscopes help them find very small clues.

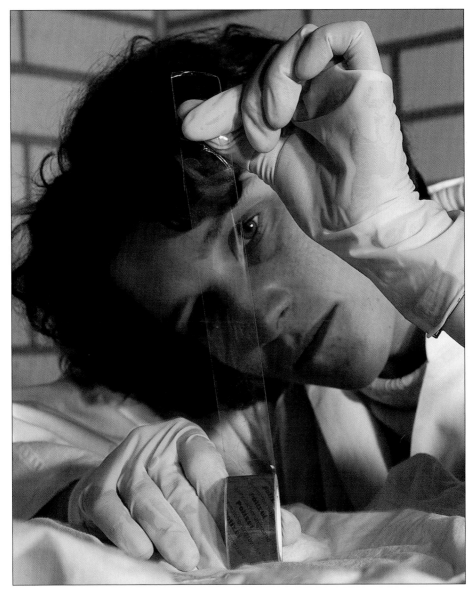

21

Some scientists study how people lived a long time ago. They use microscopes, too. They look for tiny clues in the dirt.

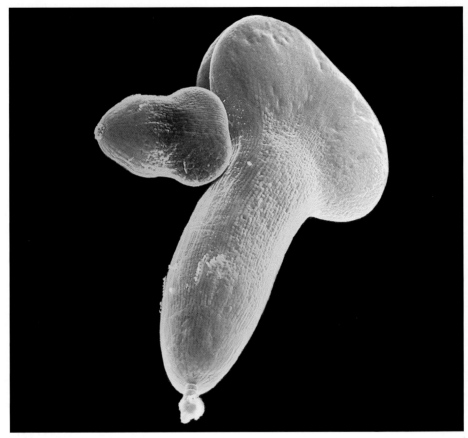

Turnip seed

They may find seeds that
tell what people ate.

They may find bits of cloth
that tell what people wore.

Cloth

Other kinds of scientists use microscopes, too. Some study rocks. Others study things that live in the water.

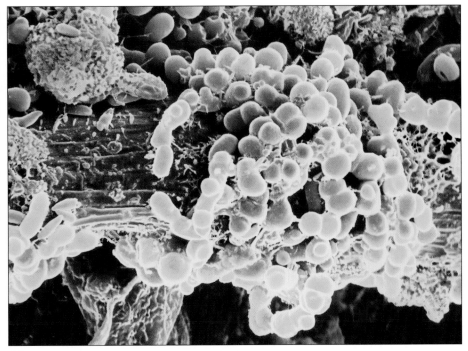
Algae

Algae (AL-jee) are small plants that live in the water. Sometimes you can only see them with a microscope.

This is what your blood looks like through a microscope.

A microscope lets us see a whole different world.

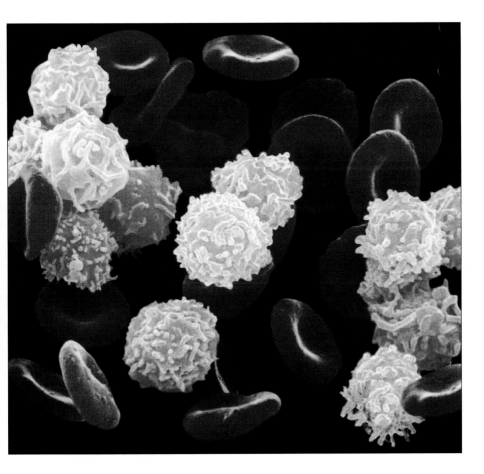

Words You Know

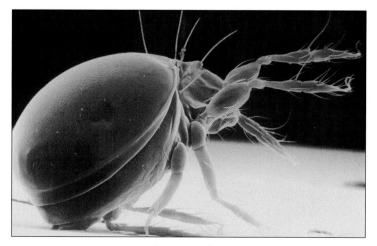

dust mite

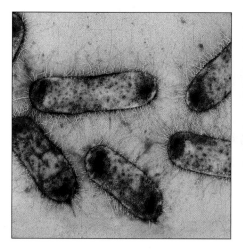

germs

insect

microscope

scientist

31

Index

About the Author

Dr. Linda Bullock lives in Austin, Texas, where she works as a writer and editor. Dust bunnies live under her desk.

Photo Credits

Photographs © 2003: Corbis Images: 8 (Bob Krist), 7, 31 top (Ariel Skelley); Dwight R. Kuhn Photography: 11 top; James Levin: cover; Peter Arnold Inc.: 22 (Heinz Plenge), 5, 12 (David Scharf), 21 (Volker Steger); Photo Researchers, NY: 18 (Beranger/BSIP/SS), 24, 25 (Dr. Jeremy Burgess/SPL), 9 (Deep Light Productions/SPL), 13 (Christian Gautier/Jacana), 17 (Oliver Meckes), 11 bottom, 19, 30 bottom left (Meckes/Ottawa), 27 (Microfield Scientific LTD/SPL); Randy Matusow: 3, 4; Visuals Unlimited: 14 (Gary Gaugler), 15, 29, 30 top (David M. Phillips), 26, 31 bottom (Science/ARS), 10, 30 bottom right (Jonathan D. Speer).